Networking Like a Pro

Create Lasting Connections for Success

Table of Contents

Chapter 1. Introduction

In our dynamic Special Report, "Networking Like a Pro: Create Lasting Connections for Success," we delve into the exciting world of successful networking. This isn't a technical manual, but rather your all-access backstage pass to the vibrant world of professional connection-building. This report is your cheerful guide to becoming an absolute networking maestro, jam-packed with proven strategies, expert insights, and candid anecdotes from successful networkers. By the end of the report, you'll have the confidence and skills to weave a robust network that can propel your career and personal growth to unimaginable heights. This isn't just another report—it's the launchpad for your new, interconnected future. Get ready for a fantastic journey that will transform you into the networker you've always aspired to be!

Chapter 2. Understanding the Power of Networking

If you've ever heard the phrase, "It's not what you know, but who you know," you have an inkling of just how powerful networking can be. Behind this simple phrase lie multifaceted layers of truth that underline the importance and ubiquity of networking in our professional and personal lives.

2.1. Understanding Networking

Fundamentally, networking is about creating and nurturing relationships. It involves meeting and getting to know people who you can assist, and who can potentially assist you in return. Your network includes everyone from friends and family to work colleagues and members of groups to which you belong.

Think about the last time you found a job. Did you find the posting on a job board, or was it through someone you knew? Perhaps you were introduced to your current partner through a mutual acquaintance. Our lives are deeply intertwined with the lives of those around us, and those connections form a network that constantly shapes and reshapes our paths.

2.2. The Benefits of Networking for Career Success

If networking has become a buzzword in the professional world, it is with good reason. Strengthening your networking skills and becoming an active participant in your network can provide a litany of benefits.

A broad network can open doors to new opportunities. When

openings occur, they'll often be filled by people within the network. The more people you are connected with, the more likely it is that you'll discover these opportunities. A robust network also enhances your learning and development. It provides you a plethora of perspectives, broadens your knowledge, and offers countless opportunities for insights.

Moreover, networking can be a source of support during challenging times. The people within your network can provide encouragement and offer advice based on their experiences.

2.3. Subtle Power of Networking

You may ask, what makes networking maintain such an indomitable hold over our career and life success? The answer lies in its subtlety.

Networking works in the background, gently shaping our interactions and opportunities. It is a slow process and involves more listening than talking, and more giving than taking. Only when a tree bears fruit do we think about all the sunshine, rain, and fertilizer that got it to that point.

2.4. Tools for Effective Networking

Networking is a skill, and like any other skill, it can be developed with practice. Active listening is an essential tool. Most people love talking about themselves, but fewer are good listeners. Practice listening more than you speak, and when you do speak, ask thoughtful questions based on what you've heard.

Learning how to talk about yourself is also essential. It's not a question of bragging about your achievements but sharing what you do, what interests you, and what you're working on.

Another valuable tool is consistency. Networking is not something that you can do once and forget about. It requires consistent effort, following up after meetings, remembering details about people, and staying in touch even when you don't need anything.

2.5. Networking in the Digital Age

In today's interlinked world, digital networking plays a crucial role. Social media platforms like LinkedIn, Twitter, Facebook, and countless others offer immense opportunities for networking. However, these platforms should augment, rather than replace, face-to-face networking.

The importance of engaging genuinely and warmly, whether online or offline, cannot be overstated. The power of networking lies as much in its humanity as in its spreadsheets and social media accounts.

To sum up, networking involves building relationships based on mutual aid and reciprocity. It's a two-way street. Thus, don't approach networking as a process of using people for your own gain, but rather as a way of growing together. The power of networking lies in the power of community. By understanding this, you stand better positioned to set off on your networking journey, building lasting connections that help craft not only your career success but also your personal growth.

Chapter 3. The Art of Effective Communication

Effective communication forms the backbone of successful networking. It's the golden thread that weaves together the fabric of your professional relationships. Nurture it well and watch your network flourish.

3.1. The Power of Active Listening

Active listening is the first step towards effective communication. This doesn't mean simply waiting for your turn to talk. Active Listening translates to fully concentrating, understanding, responding to, and then remembering what's being said.

Think about your approach when you're in a conversation. If you're fixated on waiting for an opportunity to speak or mentally preparing your response before the speaker has even finished, you're not providing them the full attention that they deserve. Understand that good listeners have a unique charisma – they make people feel heard and valued. It's through this magnetism that lasting connections are cultivated.

To practice active listening:

- Maintain comfortable eye contact.

- Avoid distractions or picking up your phone.

- Nod and show affirmative body language to show understanding.

- Provide feedback by summarizing their points and asking relevant questions.

3.2. The Clarity of Message Construction

An equally important counterpart of effective communication revolves around your ability to clearly express your thoughts. Your goal should be to articulate your ideas in a simple, concise, and articulate way.

This starts with the mental organization. Using clear language and accurate grammar constructs an easily understandable narrative. Try presenting your ideas in a logical sequence and avoid using jargon unless necessary.

One common method is the "KISS" rule—Keep It Simple and Straightforward. Zig Ziglar, a famous American author, and motivational speaker once said, "If you can't explain it to a six-year-old, you don't understand it yourself." This quote really brings forth the essence of simplicity in communication.

3.3. Tuning Into Nonverbal Cues

While words convey meaning, nonverbal cues convey sentiments. These nonverbal cues—such as body language, facial expressions, gestures, and tone of voice—constitute a significant part of the communication process.

Understanding and correctly interpreting these signals can provide a greater insight into the thoughts and feelings of others. Simultaneously, being aware of your own nonverbal cues helps ensure that your communication is congruent and clear.

Hints to grasp nonverbal communication better:

- Maintain an open posture, which signals openness and receptiveness.

- Pay attention to your tone, as it can greatly impact the perception of your message.

- Facial expressions, especially eye contact, should align with your spoken words.

3.4. Mastering the Art of Persuasion

Persuasion is an essential communication skill in the networking world. It's about influencing individuals or groups towards considering your ideas or services. It's not about high-pressure sales tactics, but a subtle blend of confidence, passion, and logical argumentation.

Influence becomes easy when there's trust established. Hence, ethical persuasion should always aim at a mutually beneficial outcome. The principles laid by Dr. Robert Cialdini in "Influence: The Psychology of Persuasion," provide an excellent guide for delivering persuasive communication:

1. Reciprocity: People tend to return favors.

2. Commitment and Consistency: People want to act consistently with their values and commitments.

3. Social Proof: People tend to follow others.

4. Liking: People are easily persuaded by individuals they like.

5. Authority: People respect authority, expertise, and credibility.

6. Scarcity: Items and opportunities become more desirable when they are limited.

Remember, the aim of persuasive communication isn't to manipulate but to create a win-win situation.

3.5. Technological Nuances of Communication

In our digital age, networking isn't confined to face-to-face interactions. Emails, video conferencing, and social networking sites are now essential parts of the networking landscape. Thus, mastering the art of online communication is imperative to manage these digital interactions successfully.

In this context, relevant points to bear in mind include:

- Being courteous and professional.
- Tailoring your communication style to the medium you're using.
- Respecting time zones and response times.
- Being mindful of etiquette in virtual meetings.

Effective communication fuels successful networking. It's an art that demands continuous refining and practicing. As you start focusing on these aspects and practice them consciously during your conversations, you'll notice that not only are your professional relationships becoming stronger, but also your personal growth is expanding. Keep honing these assets; soon, you'll possess a network that's not only robust but also rewarding and fulfilling!

Chapter 4. Building Relationships, Not Just Contacts

Creating meaningful relationships is the heart and soul of networking. A networking maestro understands that it's not about handing out business cards or adding records to a contact list—it's about forming partnerships that transcend the typical definition of a contact and evolve into true connections. We'll explore a myriad of methods to form, cultivate, and sustain these relationships, while also helping you understand the difference between having contacts and networking connections.

4.1. Understanding The Objective

To build relationships, you must first understand the aim of networking. It is all about relationship building and cultivating a connection that goes beyond a mere professional acquaintance. You should seek to foster mutual respect and trust. It's not about creating transactional relationships; it's about establishing goodwill and cooperation. It might be helpful to start viewing networking as a lifelong endeavor rather than a means to an immediate end. The key is to make connections before you need them.

Remember, people connect with people, not with business cards, LinkedIn profiles, or fancy titles. So, your goal in networking should be to create a sincere connection that gives the other party as much value as it gives you.

4.2. Forming Genuine Connections

Building relationships rather than contacts is about authenticity and engagement. Here are some strategies:

1. **Get Personal**: Going beyond business topics and showing interest in the person you're networking with helps to forge more profound connections. Understand their interests, their background, and their ambitions. However, respect personal boundaries—make the conversation about them and not intrusive.

2. **Listen Actively**: Show that you're as interested in giving your attention as receiving it. It's not merely about waiting for your turn to speak. Show interest, make eye contact, and give visible cues to indicate your attention and involvement in the conversation.

3. **Offer Value**: This isn't about immediate material exchange. It can be as simple as sharing a relevant piece of information, a job update, or even an introduction to another contact. The idea is to become a resource to your network members and establish reciprocity, which is a crucial foundation for any relationship.

4.3. Cultivating the Relationship

After forming an initial connection, cultivate it to foster a relationship. Remember, if you're not nurturing your connections, you're not networking—you're just collecting contacts.

1. **Follow up**: After making the initial connection, always take the time to follow up. It could be a simple email saying you enjoyed the conversation, sharing an interesting article related to your discussion or suggesting a further meeting.

2. **Set Regular Interactions**: Maintain regular communication to help the relationship thrive. It's about creating continuous touchpoints that keep you relevant and fresh in each other's minds. It can be through emailing, video calls, or face-to-face meetings.

3. **Support without expectations**: One of the hallmarks of a robust networking relationship is offering help without expecting anything in return. This selfless characteristic creates a bond trust and makes the relationship meaningful.

4.4. Sustaining a Networking Relationship

Once you've created and cultivated these relationships, the next challenge is sustainability. A good relationship is built on consistent efforts and mutual benefits. Here's how to toll the line:

1. **Keep the dialogue alive**: Regular conversations are a powerful tool. Reach out during holidays, birthdays, work anniversaries, or just to catch up. This keeps the relationship active.

2. **Offer and ask for help**: Strengthen your relationships by offering your assistance periodically and don't hesitate to ask for aid when necessary. This transaction creates a healthy balance.

3. **Be patient**: Relationships take time to develop. Be patient and let the connections grow naturally.

The difference between having a 'friend' and an 'acquaintance' in the networking world lies in the relationship quality. An acquaintance might assist you out of obligation, while a friend will gladly help because they value your relationship. The journey to reaching that 'friend' level might seem overwhelming, but with these strategies, it becomes manageable and almost second nature.

Understand that networking is about quality over quantity. Aim to enrich your influence circle with connections that are meaningful to you and the ones that stimulate your professional growth. In the world of networking, relationships are the best currency—learn to invest in people, and the returns will be manifold.

Chapter 5. Mastering Social Media for Professional Networking

In today's digital world, social media has metamorphosed from a mere recreational activity to a vital networking tool for professionals. Harnessing the power of social media for networking can help you establish a strong brand, connect with like-minded individuals, discover job opportunities, and generate leads.

5.1. Understanding Each Platform's Purpose

First and foremost, it's pivotal to comprehend that each social media platform serves a different purpose and attracts diverse demographics. Every platform has unique features that make it suitable for distinct networking tactics. Understanding these distinctions will guide your online networking strategy.

LinkedIn is everyone's go-to platform for professional networking. Craft your profile into an articulate, compelling mini-resume and stay active. Connect with colleagues, join industry-specific groups and actively participate to stay on the radar. LinkedIn also provides an opportunity for publishing articles, enhancing your exposure and position as an industry thought leader.

Twitter might seem informal, but it's a potent tool to connect with professionals, influencers, and companies worldwide. Regularly tweeting about industry trends, insights, and your day-to-day can increase your interaction with your connections. Remember to leverage hashtags to expand content reach.

Facebook allows connecting with colleagues and friends on a personal level while its Groups feature can facilitate professional connections and discussions. A word of caution: keep your profile polished as potential employers tend to check Facebook profiles.

Instagram is a visually-oriented platform where you can depict your professional life, brand, and interests through photos. Instagram Stories and Instagram Live are great tools for engaging with your audience in a real-time, interactive way.

5.2. Crafting an Effective Online Persona

Building an attractive online persona is more than just a profile picture and bio; it involves every interaction, every post, even the aesthetics of your posts. Incorporating industry keywords in your bio can work wonders for your visibility. Maintaining a consistent online persona across all social media platforms can foster recognition and trust among your connections.

5.3. Creating Quality Content

Content is king when it comes to establishing your voice in the online sphere. Sharing quality content not only increases your visibility but also demonstrates your knowledge and passion, thereby attracting like-minded professionals. Create a content calendar to ensure a consistent posting schedule. Always welcome engagement on your posts by responding to comments, provoking discussions and connecting with others who share similar content.

5.4. Leveraging Hashtags, Mentions, and Direct Messages

Hashtags are a useful tool for getting your content discovered. By adding relevant hashtags, you enhance the chances of being discovered by individuals or businesses looking for content in your field. Similarly, tagging or mentioning others, especially influencers, can lead to engagement or potential partnerships. Direct messaging provides an ideal opportunity to forge personal connections, but remember to be respectful and professional.

5.5. Networking Through Groups and Communities

Joining groups and communities in your field paves the way for interacting with professionals who share the same interests. These spaces offer opportunities to learn, share knowledge, engage in fruitful discussions and find potential collaborators or employers. Being active and consistent in such groups elevates your chances of being noticed.

5.6. Monitoring Your Progress

There's no way to truly grasp the effectiveness of your strategies without monitoring your metrics. Keep an eye on your engagement rate, follower count, and other key indicators to understand how well your social media networking is working.

5.7. Going Beyond the Digital - Making Connections Real

Remember that the ultimate aim of online networking is to forge genuine connections that transcend the digital realm. Whenever possible, take your online connections offline by arranging face-to-face meetings, phone calls, or attending industry events. This switch can lay the foundation for long-lasting professional relationships.

In conclusion, social media has emerged as a crucial tool for professional networking. Mastering its techniques is no longer optional but necessary for every professional. Though it might appear daunting initially, with savvy strategies and persistent efforts, you can transform these platforms into your networking powerhouses and open doors to innumerable opportunities.

Chapter 6. Networking Events: How to Stand Out in the Crowd

To truly leverage the power of networking, you need to master the art of standing out at networking events. Today's networking arena is a busy, boisterous space, making it imperative for you to shine through. To that end, we've curated a compendium of tactics, insights, and anecdotes in this chapter that will equip you to be visible, memorable, and impactful at any networking event—Standing out isn't just about showcasing your skills; it's an intricate dance of professionalism, personality, and purpose that underscores your entire networking journey.

6.1. Preparation: Laying the Foundation

Your first step to standing out is robust preparation. This underscores everything—from being well-informed about the event to knowing your objectives for the occasion.

Research the Event: Master the basics—who are the hosts, what's the organization's background, who are the key attendees, what are the event's key themes? This background knowledge will help you engage in more meaningful conversations at the event and impress others by your preparation.

Know Your Objectives: Assess your reasons for attending—Are you there to meet specific individuals, to learn about specific fields or trends, or to merely expand your professional circle? Having clear goals will guide your actions and conversations during the event, helping you leave a lasting impression.

Prepare Your Pitch: Develop a succinct and compelling self-introduction that encapsulates who you are and what you offer. Remember, the goal is to pique interest, not to cover your entire professional history.

6.2. Attire: Dressing to Impress

Dress codes send a powerful subliminal message about your professionalism. Dress appropriately for the event—When in doubt, lean toward the side of caution, opting for business attire.

Here's a quick tip: Wear something memorable yet subtle. It could be a tie with an interesting pattern, a unique piece of jewelry, or even vibrant socks peeking under your pants. These can be good conversation starters and serve to make you more memorable.

6.3. Mastering the Room: Making a Lasting Impression

Now that you've laid a secure foundation and are dressed to impress, it's time to dive into the heart of the event. Here's how you can ensure you don't just blend into the crowd.

Body Language: Carrie, a veteran networker, says, "Your body language speaks long before you actually do." So, maintain eye contact, offer a firm handshake, keep an open posture, and always wear a pleasant smile.

Active Listening: A key aspect of being memorable is showing genuine interest in what others are saying. Practice active listening, which means fully concentrating, understanding, responding, and then remembering what's being said.

Offer Value: Networking isn't just about what you can gain—it's an exchange of value. Be ready and open to offer assistance, share insights, or connect individuals who could benefit from knowing each other.

Follow Up: One of the most often overlooked aspects of networking is the follow-up—it's crucial to solidify the connections you make. After the event, connect with the individuals you met via LinkedIn or email. Craft personalized messages referencing points from your discussions.

6.4. Networking Don'ts: Pitfalls to Avoid

Networking events aren't your traditional social gatherings, and it's essential to steer clear of some potential pitfalls.

Don't Dominate Conversations: Keep the conversation balanced. Don't monopolize the discussion; allow the other person to share their thoughts and experiences.

Don't Be A Card Distributor: Handing out your business cards mindlessly won't serve your purpose at a networking event. Aim for meaningful conversations, and then offer your cards.

Don't Mix Business with Drinking: While some networking events may offer alcoholic drinks, it's crucial to keep in check so as not to harm your professional impression.

Don't Forget Manners: Always respect the personal space and time of others. Don't barge into ongoing conversations or stick to one person the entire evening.

Networking events are your tickets to a world filled with potential connections, opportunities, and experiences. They provide the stage for you to showcase your talents, vision, and professional value proposition. By prepping adequately, dressing appropriately, mastering interpersonal skills, and avoiding certain don'ts, you can be sure to stand out.

Remember, networking isn't a one-time operation; these events are merely stepping stones in your larger journey towards becoming a networking maestro—a journey orchestrated through patience, persistence, and a genuine interest in building mutual relationships. And remember: you are not alone in your journey. Maurice, a successful entrepreneur and networker adds, "In the networking ecosystem, we all are learners. With every interaction, there's something new to discover and a new connection to cherish."

By effectively standing out at networking events, you not only underline your distinct personality but also strengthen your networking capability—a capability that accelerates your journey towards success in the interconnected world of today.

Chapter 7. Maximizing LinkedIn: A Networking Powerhouse

In the era of digital events and online conferences, the relevance of LinkedIn, one of the world's largest professional networks, must not be overlooked. As a networking powerhouse, this platform has grown to become an indispensable tool for fostering professional relationships, finding exciting opportunities, and expanding one's influence and reach.

7.1. Mastering Your LinkedIn Profile

Creating a compelling LinkedIn profile is the first step to successful networking on the platform. Ideally, your profile should serve as an executive summary of your professional life, showcasing your skills, experience, projects, and accomplishments. Remember, potential connections view your profile as a reflection of your brand—you, so be sure to ensure its authenticity and professionalism.

Begin by choosing the right profile picture, something crisp and professional that will be instantly recognizable. Your headline should succinctly summarize your professional identity, role, or aspiration. Don't be afraid to incorporate relevant keywords or industry buzzwords—it's a simple way to increase your visibility in search results.

Your summary section is where you get the chance to tell your story in your own words. Express your professional purpose, your career achievements, areas of expertise, and the kind of opportunities you are seeking or open to. Use this space to humanize yourself—inject some personality into your pitch.

Experience, education, and skills endorsement sections on LinkedIn allow you to showcase your professional pedigree and achievements. Be thorough, ensure your stated experiences align with your headline and summary, and the skills you list are relevant to your professional reputation.

7.2. Utilizing LinkedIn Features

LinkedIn offers a plethora of networking features that can help you connect with professionals globally.

- "LinkedIn Groups" provides a space for professionals in the same industry or with similar interests to share their insights, ask questions, and foster meaningful relationships. Find groups that align with your professional interests, actively participate in discussions, and leverage opportunities to show thought leadership.

- "LinkedIn Posts" are an excellent way to share industry blog posts, articles, or insights that are valuable to your connections and followers. This not only keeps your profile active but also positions you as a thought leader in your field.

- "LinkedIn Pulse" is the platform's publishing feature that allows you to write and post articles directly on LinkedIn. This tool is excellent for sharing expert knowledge, unique perspectives, and experiences.

- "LinkedIn Jobs" is not just for job seekers but for network building too. By observing the job postings in your industry, you can gain insight into the skills and qualifications companies are currently seeking, thus helping you tailor your skill-building or re-skilling efforts.

7.3. Building Your LinkedIn Network

When you send a connection request, always accompany it with a personalized message. Not only does it keep your pitch more memorable, but it also shows that you are genuinely interested, increasing the chances of your request being accepted.

It's essential to nurture the relationships you build on LinkedIn. Engage with your connections by liking, commenting, and sharing their posts. This engagement keeps you visible on their news feed and illustrates that you value what they share.

LinkedIn's advanced people search feature allows you to find people based on the company they work for, the university they went to, the industry they're in, and much more. Use this feature to strategically expand your network with professionals that align with your interests and goals.

7.4. Leveraging LinkedIn for Thought Leadership

LinkedIn's publishing platform and the ability to share posts allow you to create and share content – a cornerstone in demonstrating thought leadership. Consider posting articles, blog posts, or white papers that discuss industry trends, challenges, or your own experiences.

Always aim to add value with your content—whether you're sparking intellectual discussions or providing solutions to common professional problems, your aim should be to build a reputation where your connections look forward to your insightful updates.

7.5. Maximizing LinkedIn for Career Growth

With a network of industry professionals at your fingertips, LinkedIn can remarkably assist your career growth. By attending virtual events and webinars promoted on LinkedIn, you can network with industry leaders, learn about the industry's latest trends and developments, and perhaps stumble upon opportunities for collaboration.

Implement these tactics carefully, and your LinkedIn presence can become a powerhouse for networking, establishing thought leadership, and accelerating your career and personal growth. Networking is about fostering relationships; the more you engage with others, the more they'll engage with you—propelling your professional journey to unimaginable new heights.

Chapter 8. Maintaining Authenticity in Professional Interactions

To be an effective networker, it's crucial we remain authentic in our professional interactions. While it's natural to want to put our best foot forward, being genuine, open, and accessible remains the cornerstone to building lasting relationships. So, let's delve into the factors that contribute to an authentic approach while navigating professional networks.

8.1. The Foundation of Authenticity

The foundation of authenticity is essentially being true to who you are. This involves shedding any pretense, refraining from over-promising on skills and abilities, and being honest about your intentions. It's the ability to present your true personality, values, and beliefs without fear of being misunderstood or negatively perceived.

When interacting with others, don't be afraid to show your vulnerabilities and admit when you're uncertain or don't know something. Contrary to popular belief, our vulnerabilities often make us more relatable and can foster deeper interpersonal connections. Additionally, openly acknowledging where your knowledge or expertise ends shows a high level of self-awareness and humility—traits that are often revered in the professional world.

8.2. Constructive Honesty

Being genuine in your professional interactions also necessitates a strong dedication to honesty. This goes beyond not telling lies—it means giving constructive feedback, stating your true thoughts and opinions (while exercising tact and respect), and avoiding exaggerated flattery or false enthusiasm.

Constructive honesty is the balancing act of delivering the truth without hurting someone's feelings or damaging a relationship. Over time and with consistent practice, you will find a style and approach to honesty that is both authentic and appropriate for your professional context.

8.3. Non-Verbal Cues for Authenticity

Our words represent only a fraction of our overall communication. Non-verbal cues—such as body language, eye contact, and facial expressions—play an equally, if not more important, role in conveying authenticity. When congruent with verbal communication, non-verbal cues can strengthen the perception of authenticity.

Non-verbal cues that suggest authenticity include maintaining smooth and natural eye contact, exhibiting open body language, and adaptively mirroring the other's behaviors. While these cues can be conscious efforts, true authenticity comes when they align naturally with your verbal message, without any need for forced behavior.

8.4. Genuine Professional Interest

Having authentic interest in the people with whom you interact is another crucial ingredient in maintaining authenticity. This means not simply focusing on what others can do for you, but gaining a deep and genuine interest in who they are as individuals and professionals.

Approach conversations with curiosity and an intention to learn and grow. Try shifting your mind from a transactional networking model to a relationship-building one. This attitude change can significantly enhance the quality and depth of your interactions—leading to more resonating and enduring connections.

8.5. Delivering on Commitments

Authentic individuals are consistent and reliable, which means they stick to their commitments and follow through on promises. Being reliable fosters trust and loyalty, which are pivotal for lasting professional relationships.

In your networking interactions, make commitments carefully. Once you've committed, do what it takes to fulfill these promises. Nothing erodes trust or damages your reputation faster than unkept promises.

By embracing these principles, you can navigate the landscape of professional networking while maintaining your authenticity. Authentic individuals are admired and respected for their candiffdence and genuine approach to relationships. This reputation can provide a powerful boost to your networking endeavors, leading to stronger, more meaningful connections that can push your career and personal life to new heights. Remember the essence of networking is not about winning or losing, but about growing together and positive co-evolution.

Stay true to your values and beliefs even as you adapt to new environments, cultures, and practices. Build relationships on the principles of mutual respect, understanding, and benefit. This is the art of authentic networking—an unending journey of learning, connecting, and growing.

Chapter 9. The Follow-Up: Nurturing and Growing Your Connections

Cultivating new connections is only the first step in networking. The real work—and reward—comes from nurturing and growing those connections over time. It's not just about making acquaintances; it's about building meaningful and mutually beneficial relationships. So, how do we follow-up effectively, sustaining the relationship without coming across as too pushy or inauthentic?

9.1. The Artfulness of a Proper Follow-Up

Making an excellent first impression is, of course, a crucial start to new professional relationships. However, it is the consistent communication afterward that solidifies bonds and promotes growth. A follow-up is more than a "nice to meet you" email or a LinkedIn connection request. Instead, it's the beginning of an ongoing relationship-building process.

In the age of speedy text messages and instant replies, consider the impact of a well-crafted, thoughtful follow-up message. That email or phone call is your chance to deepen the bond formed during your initial interaction. It provides reinforcement for your shared interests and values, solidifying who you are in the other person's mind. The timing matters too. It's generally best to reach out within 48 hours post-meeting. Shortly enough to still be fresh in their memory but giving them enough space to breathe after the event or meeting.

9.2. Fine-Tuning Your Approach

While there's no one-size-fits-all follow-up strategy, certain best practices can provide a roadmap. Your approach might vary depending on the context of the initial meeting; however, the core principles remain the same.

1. Be prompt but sensible with your follow-up timing.

2. Be personal and genuine, referencing specific details from your meeting.

3. Show appreciation for their time and interactions.

4. Express your interest in keeping the conversation going.

5. Offer something of value like an article or event reference related to your conversation.

Taking these steps shows that you listened and understood during your initial conversation, reinforcing your common bonds and displaying enthusiasm to continue the relationship. But remember using a templated follow-up won't cut it. Personalization is key to success in this case.

9.3. Grace Under Pressure: Regular Communication

After your first follow-up, many struggle to maintain regular communication without feeling burdensome. The trick here is to maintain a balance: you want to stay on their radar without being intrusive. The frequency of your communication should be shaped by the depth and nature of your relationship and the industry you're in.

Take an interest in their professional activities. Congratulating them on their accomplishments or providing insights relevant to their work showcases your growing commitment to the relationship. Utilize social media platforms like LinkedIn or Twitter to stay abreast with their updates. Comment on their posts, or better yet, share their content from time to time to show your support.

9.4. Advance with Mutual Benefits

As your connection matures, strive for deeper engagements that add shared value. Perhaps this could mean collaborating on a project, inviting them to an event, introducing them to another contact, or being a sounding board for ideas.

At the end of the day, networking is about reciprocity. It's essential to look for opportunities where you can help or provide value to your connection, just as they might do for you. Remember that nurturing relationships is not merely a process of "taking" but a harmonious balance of giving and receiving.

9.5. A Long Game: Nurturing Long-Term Connections

Nurturing and growing your connections requires patience and a long-term approach. These relationships built over time can yield incalculable benefits, including mentorships, partnerships, and friendships. While following up effectively can pave the way for strong connections, remember that it's the ongoing effort and genuine interest in the other person's work and success that nurtures a lasting relationship.

Even as you meet new people and expand your network, it's critical to remember the value of sustaining long-established connections. Regular check-ins, annual coffee meetings, or the occasional email can help keep these relationships warm.

9.6. The Big Picture: Growing Your Connections

Much like a well-tended garden, your network will flourish with meaningful, deep-rooted connections if you nurture it. Remember that this is more than just a professional pursuit; it's about fostering sincere relationships that contribute to your personal and professional growth. By being attentive, genuine, and patient, you transform your rolodex of contacts into a vibrant network of opportunities waiting to get explored.

In the end, networking isn't just about expanding your connections—it's about enriching them. Whether it's by providing resources, showing support, or simply lending a listening ear, it's these small steps that nurture your network and allow it to thrive. So, dare to venture beyond the business cards and LinkedIn invites and into the world of meaningful, lasting connections. Your network—and your career—will be all the richer for it.

Chapter 10. Turning Connections into Opportunities

Mastering the art of networking, as discussed in the prior chapters, is only one part of your professional growth journey. The other, perhaps even more critical part, is learning how to turn connections into opportunities. This is where the true power of networking lies: the ability to transform an acquaintance into a business acquaintance, a friend into a collaborator, or a simple conversation into a passion project.

10.1. Establishing Rapport

The first step to converting acquaintances into opportunities is to build a rapport with them. This process should ideally start from your initial contact and continue throughout your relationship. Dialogue and shared experiences are the foundation stones of rapport. Approaching interactions with genuine interest, empathy, and open-mindedness make people more likely to trust you with their ideas, projects, or business ventures.

Effective rapport-building includes:

- Use of common language and phrases

- Shared experiences and common interests

- Open, memorable conversations

Establishing rapport is about making your connections feel comfortable and understood. It's about getting on the same wavelength and staying there.

10.2. Understanding the Needs of Your Connections

Once rapport is established, the next step would be to understand the needs and wants of your connections. Everyone you meet professionally will have different goals, targets, and expectations. By understanding what drives them, you are better positioned to provide value that aligns with their needs. This synergistic exchange can open up numerous opportunities.

Here are ways to understand the needs of your connections:

- Pay attention when they share their goals or struggles.

- Ask probing questions about their current projects or aspirations.

- Research their professional background.

The more you understand, the better equipped you'll be to turn the connection into an opportunity.

10.3. Providing Value

After you've established rapport and understood your connection's needs, it's time for you to provide value. Value can take many forms – professional advice, introductions to other networkers, resources, or simply being a good listener. What it mustn't be is a one-time affair. Providing value should be a continuous process, aimed at fostering genuine goodwill and symbiotic benefit.

Ways to provide value include:

- Sharing your expertise

- Introducing them to your other connections

- Recommending them for roles or projects that suit their skills

- Regularly providing useful resources

Remember, your aim should be to be the connection people recall when they think about their network — the one that helps, supports, and champions them.

10.4. Following Up

Follow-ups are necessary for maintaining your network. It's easy to forget someone if they don't make an effort to stay connected. Regular follow-ups help you stay on your connection's radar. While the frequency of follow-ups may vary, the importance of doing so cannot be overstated. Follow-ups can be a simple email, sharing an article relevant to their interest, congratulating them on their professional achievements, or even a casual coffee invite.

Some tips for effectual follow-ups include:

- Be relevant: Reach out with a reason, sharing relevant information or requests.

- Be regular: Aim for a balance in your outreach; neither too often nor seldom.

- Personalize your interactions: Base your follow-ups on your connection's interests or recent achievements.

10.5. From Connections to Collaborations

With rapport, understanding, value-sharing and follow-ups in place, you are primely positioned to convert your connections into collaborations. Collaborations can be professional partnerships, joint business ventures or a co-authored publication — anything which requires an amalgamation of your network's skills, knowledge and resources.

Final Thoughts:

Networking isn't merely about creating a high quantity of connections; it's about building high-quality connections that can potentially yield opportunities. With every interaction or shared experience, you are sowing the seeds for opportunities that can renew, amplify or redefine your professional outlook. Turning connections into opportunities isn't always instantaneous. It is a rich process, requiring patience, sincerity, and a strategic approach. But once mastered, its rewards can push the boundaries of what you initially thought possible.

'"Opportunities," as the old saying goes, "don't happen. You create them." By turning your connections into opportunities, you're proactively creating that brighter, more integrated future you've always aspired towards. Keep connecting, keep growing, and keep pushing forward.

Chapter 11. Continuous Learning: Refining and Expanding Your Networking Skills

Today's industry leaders don't merely survive in their fields—they thrive by continuously learning and refining their networking skills. Irrespective of your industry or the stage of your career, you should never stop acquiring knowledge, developing relationships, and expanding your horizons.

Your journey into continuous learning and networking begins now.

11.1. Acquire a Growth Mindset

A growth mindset can act as the barometer of your networking success. It's the prerequisite mental state that adapts, evolves, and never shies away from adversity. Embrace this mindset to continually learn, meet new people, and build or deepen connections.

A growth mindset involves:

1) Curiosity: Maintain a genuine interest in others, their stories, their struggles, and their victories. This curiosity can drive conversations and deepen bonds, transforming those surface-level encounters into meaningful connections.

2) Resilience: Every networking attempt won't be a slam dunk. There will be unanswered emails, awkward conversations, and missed opportunities. But with a resilient growth mindset, you see these not as failures, but as stepping stones to improvement.

3) Openness: Be open to new ideas, cultures, people, and experiences. This openness makes you approachable and can enrich your personal and professional life manifold.

11.2. Mastering the Art of Listening

Listening, often underplayed, is an axiom of successful networking. It proves that you value others' thoughts, experiences, and time. It's through listening that you comprehend and empathize, laying the groundwork for sturdy relationship-building.

Adopt these listening techniques to bolster your networking skills:

1) Active Listening: Active listeners participate fully in conversations by giving appropriate responses, asking elaborate questions, and providing relatable anecdotes. This engagement validates the speaker's ideas and encourages open dialogue.

2) Empathic Listening: Here, listeners put themselves in others' shoes to better understand and respond to their needs, wants, and emotions.

3) Appreciative Listening: Appreciation in listening is about acknowledging others' successes or viewpoints, fostering mutual respect and a deeper connection.

11.3. Elevate Your Communication Skills

Effective communication goes hand in hand with masterful networking. Besides verbal and written communication, honing non-verbal cues can greatly enhance how others perceive you.

1) Verbal Communication: Clearly articulate your thoughts, opinions, and ideas while remaining respectful and positive. Use sophisticated

but simple language to be easily understood.

2) Written Communication: Be concise and coherent in your emails, messages, and other written exchanges. Maintain a balance between professionalism and ease.

3) Non-Verbal Communication: Positive body language, such as maintaining eye contact, firm handshakes, and relaxed posture, can greatly impact networking. Be cognizant of what you're wordlessly conveying.

11.4. Nurturing Existing Relationships

While forming new connections is important, nurturing existing relationships is equally so. Regular interaction, showing appreciation, providing support, or just checking in ensures your network remains warm, appreciative, and mutually beneficial.

1) Regular Interaction: Set reminders to touch base with your connections, keep them updated, and ask about their endeavours.

2) Mutual Support: Be there for your network in times of adversity and celebrate their victories. Such support fortifies your connections.

3) Show Appreciation: A simple 'Thank You' or acknowledging their efforts can go a long way in strengthening your bond.

11.5. Exploring New Networking Avenues

In the ever-expanding landscape of professional networking, diverse platforms offer potential to connect with individuals worldwide. Leveraging these can enable you to attract diverse viewpoints, talents, and opportunities.

1) Online Networking: LinkedIn, Twitter, industry-specific forums are effective places to connect with professionals from varied backgrounds.

2) Conferences and Events: Attending conferences, seminars, and workshops within your industry can provide opportunities to meet peers, industry leaders, and potential mentors.

3) Community Service: Participating in community service enables networking in a more informal, altruistic setting, often leading to genuine connections.

11.6. Keep Evolving: Reinvent and Refine

As you progress in your professional journey, reassess your networking strategies, and adapt as necessary. Stay updated on industry trends, acquire new skills, meet new people and learn from the experiences of others.

Remember, a networking maestro is not born overnight, but through continuous learning, resilience, and evolution. To make the most of your networking journey, remind yourself that it's not just about 'what you know' but also about 'who you know.' Hence, be strategic in your approach, genuine in your conversations, and open to continuous learning and evolving.

In closing, networking isn't just about making connections—it's about making connections count. And that begins with you, the quality of your interactions, and an unyielding quest for learning. With these guiding principles, you're well on your way to refining and expanding your networking skills for unprecedented success.

Welcome to the continual process of learning and networking. Your upgraded interconnected future starts here. There's no looking back!

www.ingramcontent.com/pod-product-compliance
Lightning Source LLC
Chambersburg PA
CBHW071047260726

48661CB00007B/3185